JOHN W. SCHAUM
THEORY LESSONS
BOOK ONE

D1479598

John W. Schaum Theory Lessons

1. MUSIC THEORY FOR THE EARLIEST BEGINNER

There is a need for music theory in the earliest stages of piano study. *The John W. Schaum Theory Lessons* may begin at the very first piano lesson.

2. MIDDLE C APPROACH

These theory lessons use the middle C approach, so they correlate very closely with the actual learning steps of the early stages of piano study.

3. PERFORATED PAGES

Perforations allow the teacher to remove the lesson pages and assign them individually; the student can be working on a new page at the same time as the teacher is correcting the old page.

4. SAVES TIME

The student learns theory with a minimum of the teacher's time. Adequate explanatory remarks precede each new step so that the student can do the assignment without lengthy explanation by the teacher. The teacher can devote the majority of lesson time to the student's actual piano playing.

5. DEVELOPS STUDENT'S INITIATIVE

After reading the explanations given with each lesson, most students need no extra help from the teacher. The assignment can be prepared at home or at the lesson and left with the teacher for correction, thereby developing the student's initiative, as well as conserving valuable lesson time.

6. CLASS OR PRIVATE INSTRUCTION

The John W. Schaum Theory Lessons are suitable for class lessons as well as for private instruction.

Lesson 1. Finger Numbers

Name _____   Date _____   Grade _____

Left Hand

DIRECTIONS:
The fingers are numbered 1, 2, 3, 4, 5.
The thumb is always number 1.
Below are ten hand pictures.
Write the number of the finger that is marked with an x.

Right Hand

 The marked finger is number _____

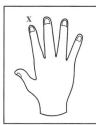 The marked finger is number _____

 The marked finger is number _____

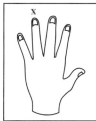 The marked finger is number _____

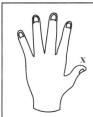 The marked finger is number _____

 The marked finger is number _____

 The marked finger is number _____

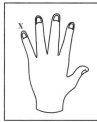 The marked finger is number _____

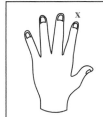 The marked finger is number _____

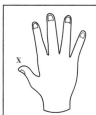 The marked finger is number _____

Lesson 2. Up and Down

Name _____ Date _____ Grade _____

There are two ways of moving at the keyboard, *up* and *down.*
From *left to right* is UP. From *right to left* is DOWN.

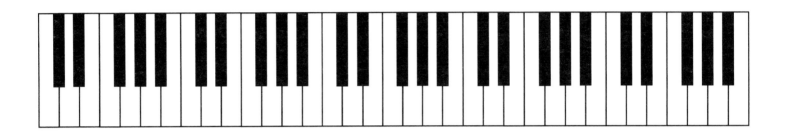

DIRECTIONS: Below is a series of hands pointing in two directions. Write UP or DOWN in each box.

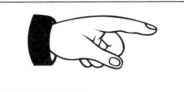

THIS WAY IS _____

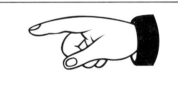

THIS WAY IS _____

THIS WAY IS _____

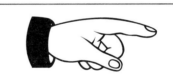

THIS WAY IS _____

THIS WAY IS _____

THIS WAY IS _____

THIS WAY IS _____

THIS WAY IS _____

Lesson 3. The Musical Alphabet *(Forward)*

Name _____   Date _____   Grade _____

The white keys of the piano are named after the first seven letters of the alphabet, and are repeated over and over on the keyboard. When we go UP, or left to right, we go in *alphabetical* order, as follows:

A   B   C   D   E   F   G   A   B   C   D   E   F   G   A   B   C   D   E   F   G   etc.

DIRECTIONS: On the keyboards below, write the white key letter names in alphabetical order. The starting letter is given on each keyboard.

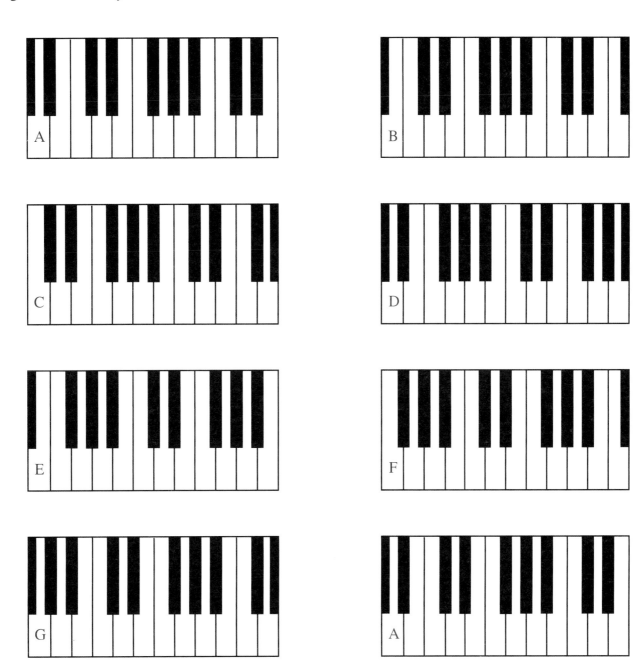

Lesson 4. The Musical Alphabet *(Backwards)*

Name _____   Date _____   Grade _____

When we go DOWN on the keyboard, we go from *right to left.* Then the letter names go *backwards,* as follows:

G F E D C B A G F E D C B A G F E D C B A etc.

DIRECTIONS: On the keyboards below, write the white key letter names *backwards.* The starting letter is given on each keyboard.

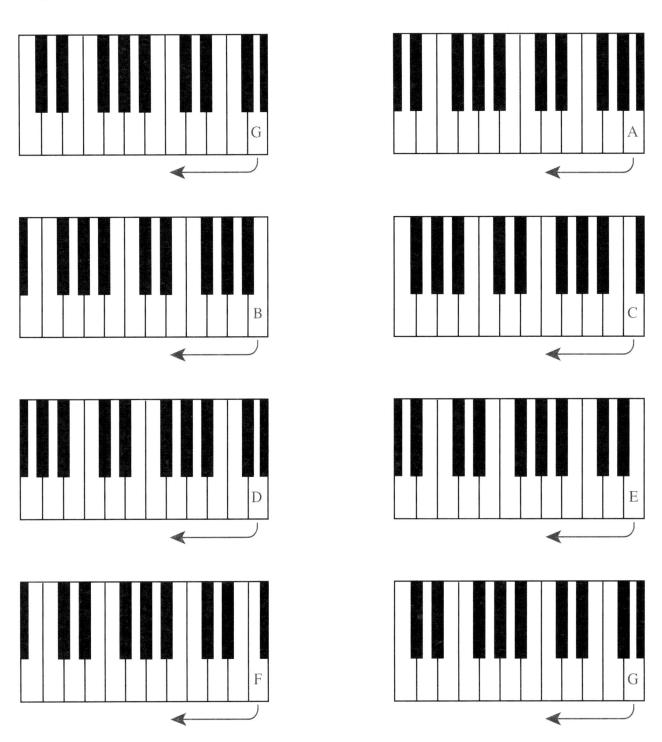

Lesson 5. Black Key Groups

Name _____   Date _____   Grade _____

DIRECTIONS: The black keys on the piano are divided into groups of twos and threes. Write the number 2 above each group of *two black keys* on the keyboard diagram below. The first group is marked as a sample.

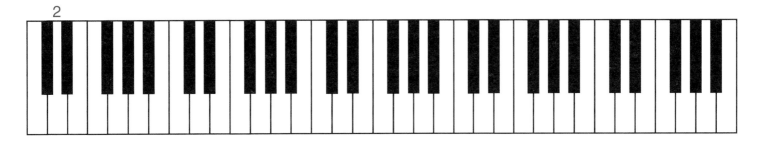

Write the number 3 above each group of *three black keys*. The first group is marked as a sample.

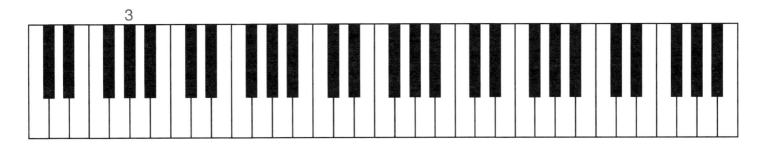

Write the number 2 or 3 above all black groups on the keyboard diagrams below.

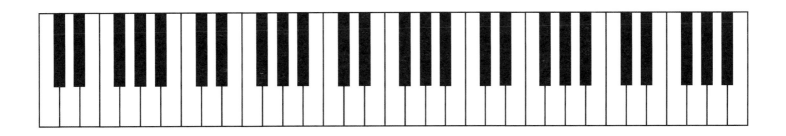

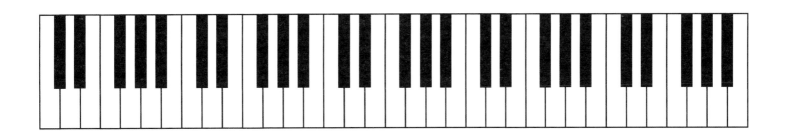

Lesson 6. White Key Names

Name _____   Date _____   Grade _____

D is an important white key to remember. It is sometimes called the sandwich note, because it is *between* two black keys. On the keyboard diagram below, write in each D. The first one is marked as a sample.

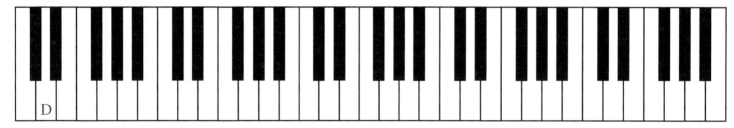

When you know where D is, you can easily find C and E because they are on either side of D. Write in each C and E on the following keyboard diagram. The first two are marked as samples.

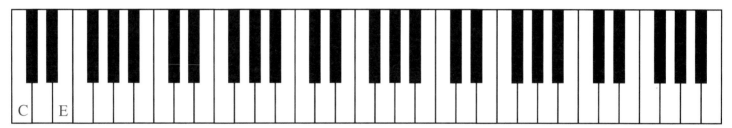

A is another important white key name. It is always found in the group of three black keys. It is the white key just before the third black key (from the left). Write in each A. The first one is marked as a sample.

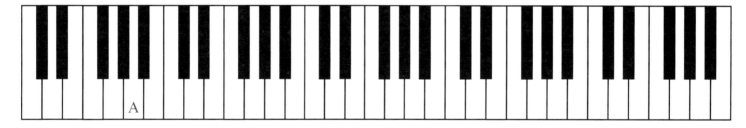

B is the first white key to the *right* of A. Write in each B on the keyboard diagram below. F and G are the white keys to the *left* of A. Write in each G. Then write in all the Fs. The first letters are marked as a sample.

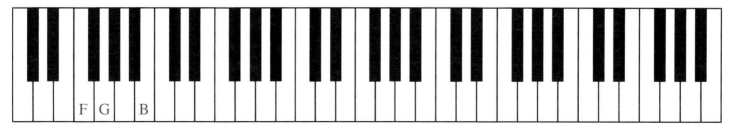

Lesson 7. Octaves

Name _____   Date _____   Grade _____

On the following keyboard diagram, all the Ds are printed in color. The distance from one D to the next D is called an OCTAVE, as indicated by the curved red lines. Likewise, from one C to the next C is an octave and from one G to the next G is an octave, and so on.

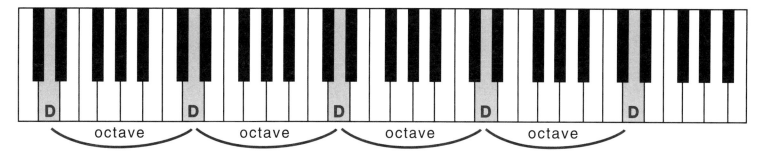

DIRECTIONS: On the keyboard chart below, color each C **<u>blue</u>** and join the C octaves with curved blue lines. Use crayon, colored pencil or ball point pen. A felt tip marker should be used only if it does not show through to the other side of the paper.

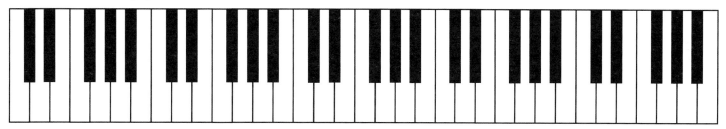

On the following keyboard chart, color each E **<u>purple</u>** and connect the E octaves with curved purple lines.

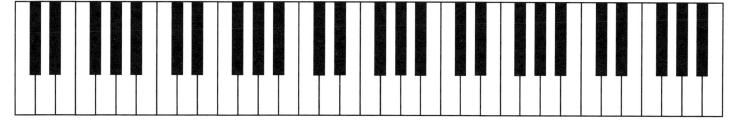

Color each A **<u>yellow</u>** and join the A octaves with curved yellow lines.

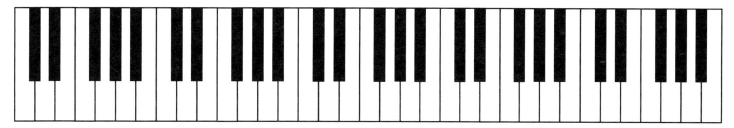

Lesson 8. More Octaves

Name _____   Date _____   Grade _____

Color each B **red** and join the B octaves with curved red lines.

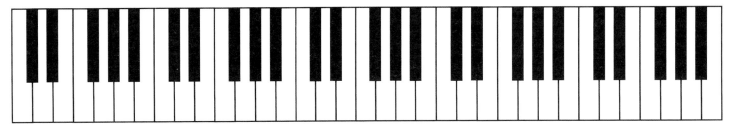

Color each G **green** and connect G octaves with curved green lines.

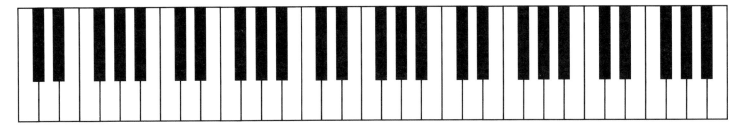

Color each F **orange** and connect F octaves with curved orange lines.

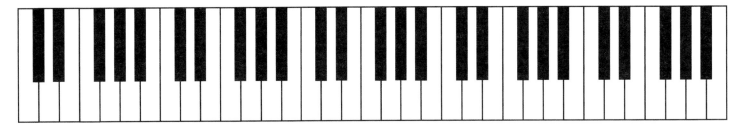

Color each D **brown** and connect D octaves with curved brown lines.

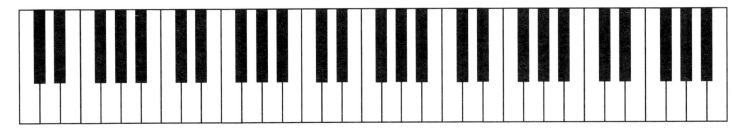

Lesson 9. The Grand Staff

Name _____   Date _____   Grade _____

Long ago, music was written on an eleven line staff.

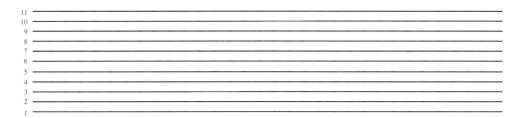

Music in those days was very difficult to read because there were so many lines and spaces. Later, the eleven line staff was split into two smaller staffs of five lines each. The middle line (where middle C was written) was removed and the upper five lines became the treble staff. The lower five lines became the bass staff.

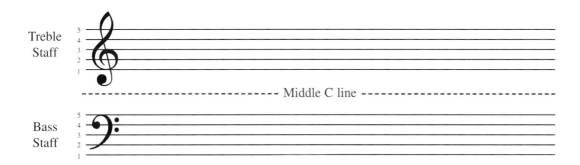

DIRECTIONS: The staffs below have both treble and bass clefs. Write U (up) on the dotted line below each *treble* clef. Write D (down) on the dotted line below each *bass* clef. See samples below.

(Samples)

Lesson 10. The Clef Signs

Name _____ Date _____ Grade _____

Clef signs are used to indicate highness or lowness on the piano. The treble clef (𝄞) usually stands for the *upper* half of the piano. The bass clef (𝄢) usually stands for the *lower* half.

The treble clef is made in the following five steps:

Trace the treble clef steps in pencil below.

Make five treble clefs according to the above directions.

The bass clef is made in the following four steps:

Trace the bass clef steps in pencil below.

Make four bass clefs according to the above directions.

EL00244A

Lesson 11. Clefs and Hands

Name _____ Date _____ Grade _____

DIRECTIONS: In piano music, the right hand usually plays notes in the treble clef and the left hand usually plays notes in the bass clef. Below is a series of hand pictures. Draw a treble clef sign (𝄞) in all right hand pictures and a bass clef sign (𝄢) in all left hand pictures.

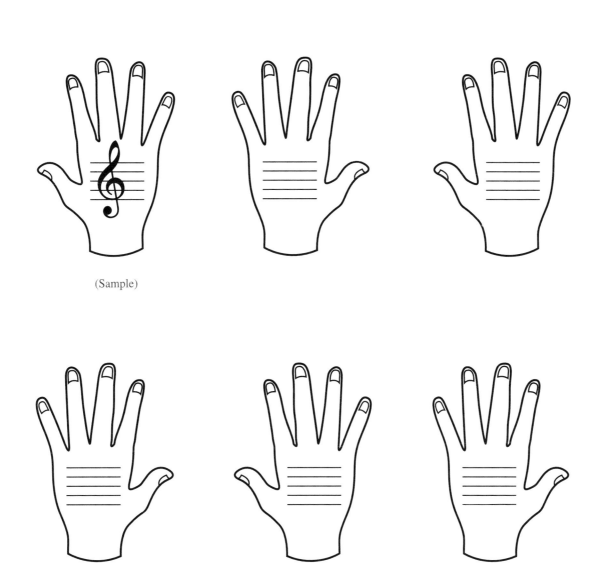

(Sample)

Write T (treble) or B (bass) under each of the following clefs.
The first is marked as a sample.

T   ....

Lesson 12. Notes on Lines and Spaces

Name _____ Date _____ Grade _____

Here are five whole notes on the FIRST line (bottom line) of the staff.
Notice that the staff line goes through the *center* of each note.

Draw four whole notes on the **2nd** staff line.
The printed note is a sample.

Draw four whole notes on the **4th** staff line.
The printed note is a sample.

Be sure each note is half above and half below the line.

Draw four whole notes on the **3rd** staff line,
as shown in the sample.

Draw four whole notes on the **5th** staff line,
as shown in the sample.

Notes in a *space* are placed *between* two staff lines.
The *first* space is between the *bottom two* staff lines.

Draw four whole notes in the **1st** space.
The printed note is a sample.

Draw four whole notes in the **3rd** space.
The printed note is a sample.

Be sure each note completely fills the space.

Draw four whole notes in the **2nd** space,
as shown in the sample.

Draw four whole notes in the **4th** space,
as shown in the sample.

EL00244A

Lesson 13. Numbers of Line Notes and Space Notes

Name _____   Date _____   Grade _____

The LINES of the staff are numbered 1-2-3-4-5, counting from the bottom up.
The line number is printed in red under each note in the staff below.

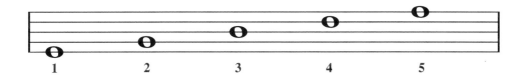

1   2   3   4   5

DIRECTIONS: Draw a whole note on the staff line indicated by each red number below. Watch carefully; the staff line should go *through the center* of the note. The note should not touch any other staff line. The first three notes are samples.

1 3 5   2 3 4   5 1 2   4 1 2

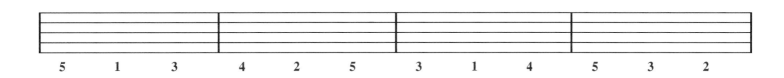

5 1 3   4 2 5   3 1 4   5 3 2

SPACES in the staff are numbered 1-2-3-4, counting from the bottom up.
The space number is printed in red under each note in the staff below.

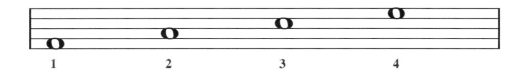

1   2   3   4

DIRECTIONS: Draw a whole note on the staff space indicated by each red number below. Watch carefully; the note should fit *between* the staff lines. The note should not go beyond the space between the two staff lines. The first three notes are samples.

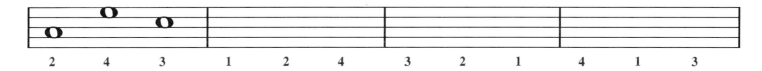

2 4 3   1 2 4   3 2 1   4 1 3

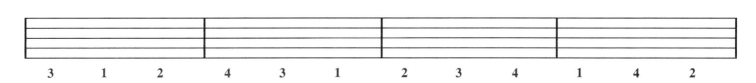

3 1 2   4 3 1   2 3 4   1 4 2

Lesson 14. Musical Alphabet in the Staff

Name _____   Date _____   Grade _____

The musical alphabet moves UP the staff in the order of lines and spaces (line-space, line-space, line-space). This is shown in the sample below.

DIRECTIONS: Write the letter name below each note. The starting note is given in each example and the other notes follow UP the musical alphabet. Notice that from letter to letter the order is always line, space, line, space, etc.

| F | G | A | B | C | | E | ---- | ---- | | C | ---- | ---- | | G | ---- | ---- |

(Sample)   (Write letter names.)

G   ----   ----   ----   ----   A   ----   ----   ----   C   ----   ----   ----

When the musical alphabet moves DOWN the staff, the alphabet goes *backwards,* as shown in the sample below.

DIRECTIONS: Write the letter name below each note. The starting note is given in each example and the other notes follow DOWN the musical alphabet (backwards).

D   C   B   A   G   F   B   ----   ----   F   ----   ----   ----

(Sample)   (Write letter names.)

E   ----   ----   ----   A   ----   ----   ----   ----   F   ----   ----   ----

E   ----   ----   ----   ----   F   ----   ----   ----   A   ----   ----

EL00244A

Lesson 15. Middle C with B and D

Name _____ Date _____ Grade _____

Middle C has its own short staff line, from the old eleven line staff (see Lesson 9). This short line is called a *leger line.*

When the middle C leger line is next to the *treble* staff, it is played with the *right* hand.

When the middle C leger line is next to the *bass* staff, it is played with the *left* hand.

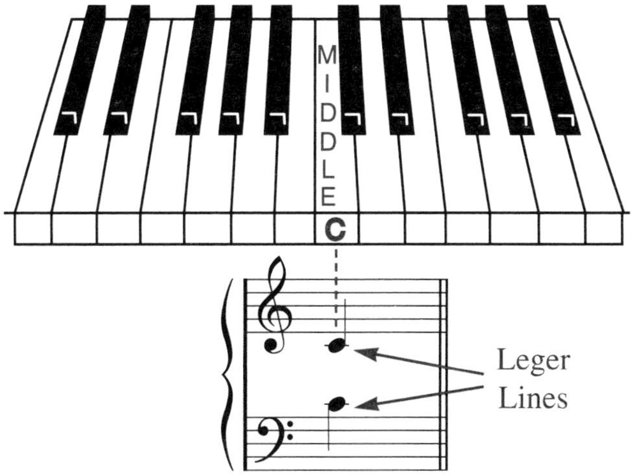

*DIRECTIONS: All of the notes below are middle C. Write R (right hand) or L (left hand) in the box below each note. See the samples below.

Leger Lines

Middle C

R   L

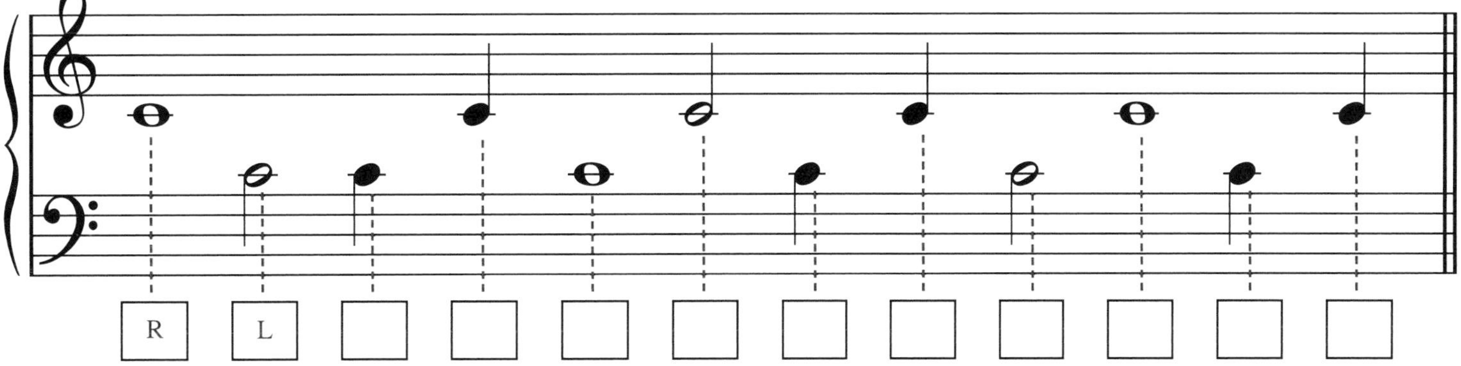

(Samples)

This keyboard diagram shows the note **B** in the bass staff along with middle C in the bass.

The diagram also shows the note **D** in the treble staff along with middle C in the treble.

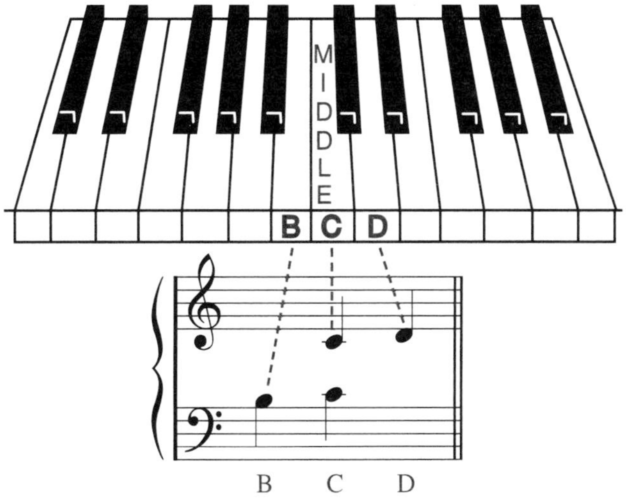

*DIRECTIONS: Study the keyboard diagram. Write the letter name B, C or D in the box below each note. See the samples below.

B   C   D

C   D

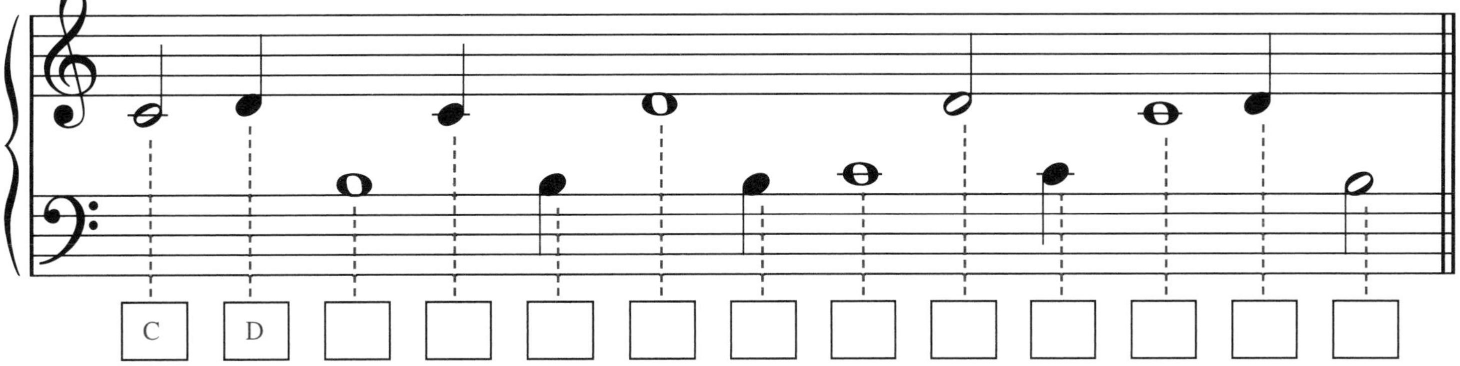

* Teacher's Note: Do not explain note values in this lesson. The object is to present middle C in many different ways so there will be a carryover into actual note reading. Note values will be presented in a later lesson.

EL00244A

Lesson 16. Middle C with A/B and D/E

Name _____   Date _____   Grade _____

In this keyboard diagram, middle C is shown with the notes A and B in the bass staff, and D and E in the treble staff.

The treble and bass staffs are joined together with a curved line called a BRACE.

*DIRECTIONS: Study the keyboard diagram in this lesson. Write the letter name A, B, C, D or E in the box below each note. See the samples below.

| C | D | | | | | | | | | |
(Samples)

* Teacher's Note: Do not explain note values in this lesson. The object is to present a mixture of different notes so there will be a carryover into actual note reading. Note values will be presented in a later lesson.

Lesson 17. Middle C with G/A/B and D/E/F

Name _____ Date _____ Grade _____

In this keyboard diagram, the note **G** is added in the bass staff. The note **F** is added in the treble staff. These two new notes are shown along with the notes presented in Lessons 15 and 16.

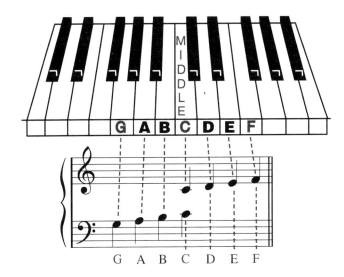

DIRECTIONS: Study the keyboard diagram. Write the letter name G, A, B, C, D, E or F in the box below each note. See the samples below.

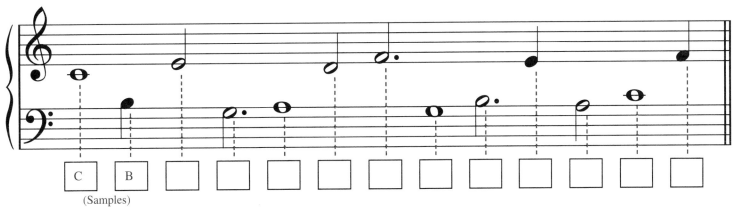

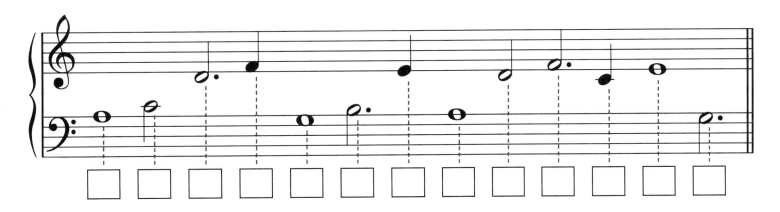

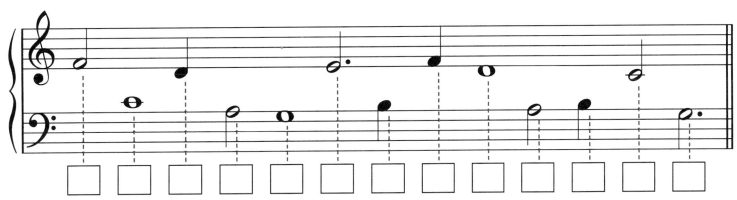

Lesson 18. Musical Spelling

Name _____ Date _____ Grade _____

DIRECTIONS: Write the correct letter name in the box below each note. You will find that the letters make words. See the sample.

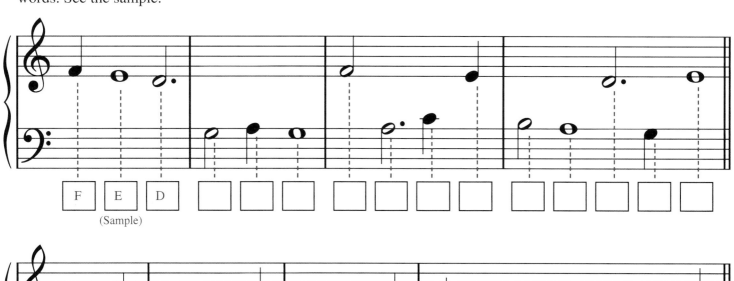

| F | E | D |
(Sample)

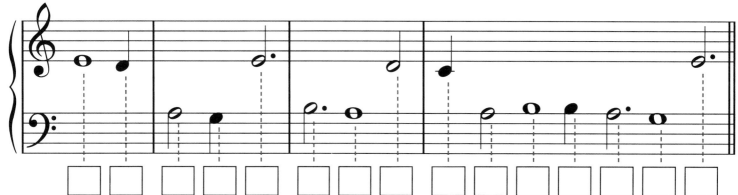

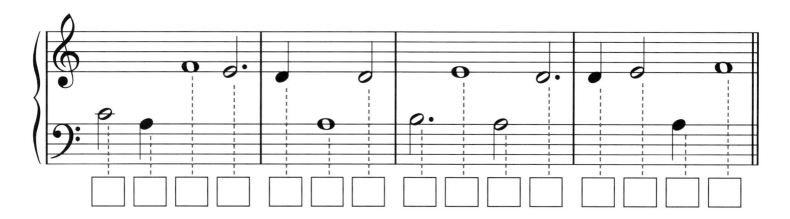

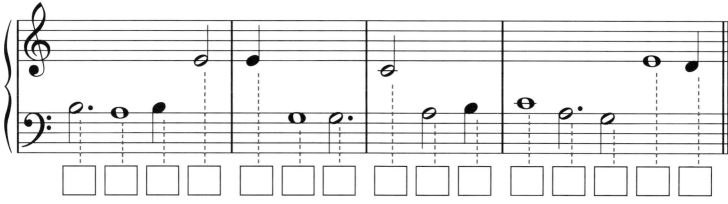

Lesson 19. Note Value Names

Name _____   Date _____   Grade _____

NOTE VALUE NAMES

These are
QUARTER NOTES
(Q)

These are
DOTTED HALF NOTES
(DH)

These are
HALF NOTES
(H)

These are
WHOLE NOTES
(W)

DIRECTIONS: Write the abbreviation for correct note value name under each of the following notes.

Q = Quarter Note   *H* = Half Note   *DH* = Dotted Half Note   *W* = Whole Note

Q   W

(Samples)

Lesson 20. Time Values

Name _____ Date _____ Grade _____

A QUARTER Note . . . . (♩) gets **1** count.

A HALF Note . . . . (♩) gets **2** counts.

A DOTTED HALF Note . . . . . . (♩.) gets **3** counts.

A WHOLE Note . . . . (o) gets **4** counts.

DIRECTIONS: How many counts does each of the following notes get?
Write the correct number below each note.

　4　　1
　----　----
　(Samples)

EL00244A

Lesson 21. Time Signatures and Counting

Name _____   Date _____   Grade _____

The two large numbers at the beginning of a staff are called the time signature. For example:

3
4

The *upper* number tells us HOW MANY counts in a measure. (In this case, 3.)

The *lower* number tells us WHAT KIND of note gets one count. (In this case, a quarter note.)

The symbol **C** is occasionally used to represent **4/4** time (common time).

DIRECTIONS: Write the counting numbers below the notes in each measure below. Be sure the numbers are *equally spaced* in each measure. The first measure is a sample.

1   2   3

(Samples)

Notice

Notice

Lesson 22. Counting in Different Time Signatures

Name _____   Date _____   Grade _____

DIRECTIONS: Write the counting numbers below the notes in each measure. Be sure the numbers are *equally spaced* in each measure. The first measure is a sample. Notice the different time signatures.

1   2   3   4

Notice

(Samples)

Notice

Notice

Lesson 23. Another Name for Each Clef

Name _____ Date _____ Grade _____

The treble clef sign (𝄞) is really a fancy G. Study the following steps and you will see.

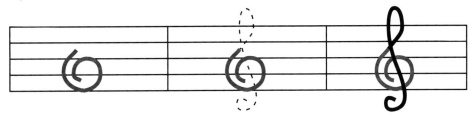

Notice that the treble clef crosses the second line of the staff (G) four times. That line gives it the name G clef.

DIRECTIONS: On the clefs below, draw heavy dots at each of the four places where the treble clef crosses the second-line G. The sample is marked correctly.

(Sample)

The bass clef sign (𝄢) is a fancy way of making F. See the following example:

Notice that the fourth line of the staff (F) is *between the two dots* of the bass clef. This is why the bass clef is also called the F clef.

DIRECTIONS: Draw lines connecting each bass clef to the two bass clef dots next to it. Notice how this makes a fancy letter F.

(Sample)

EL00244A

Lesson 24. F Clef and G Clef

Name _____   Date _____   Grade _____

DIRECTIONS: Write the letter F (for F clef) or G (for G clef) under each clef in the following lines.

G

(Sample)

DIRECTIONS: Draw a whole note G after each G clef. Draw a whole note F after each F clef.

(Sample)

DIRECTIONS: On the following staff, one treble clef (G clef) is crossed out because it is placed on the wrong line. Four more treble clefs are misplaced. Cross out the four mistakes.

(Sample)

DIRECTIONS: On the staff below, one bass clef (F clef) is crossed out because it is in the wrong place. Four more bass clefs are misplaced. Cross out the four mistakes.

(Sample)

Lesson 25. Letter Names of Notes

Name _____   Date _____   Grade _____

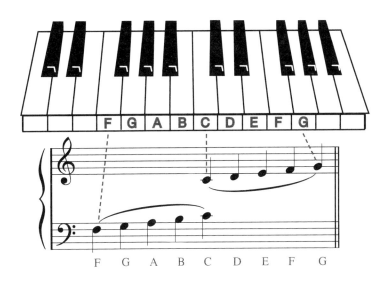

DIRECTIONS: Write the correct letter name in the box under each note. If necessary, refer to the keyboard diagram.

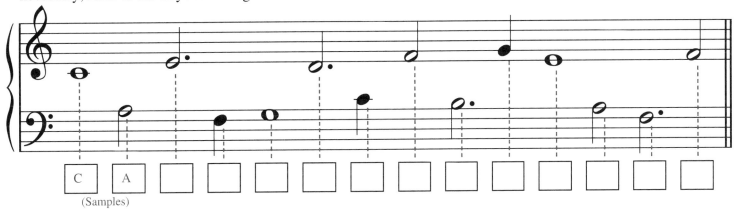

C	A												

(Samples)

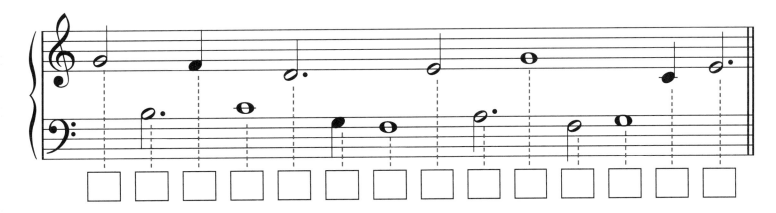

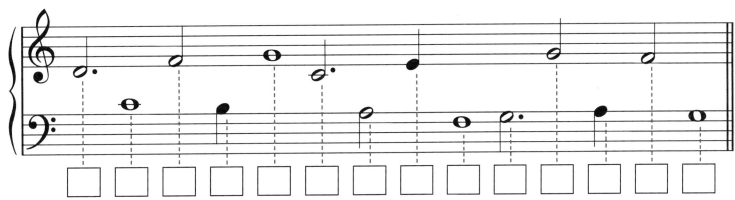

Lesson 26. Musical Spelling

Name _____ Date _____ Grade _____

* **DIRECTIONS:** Write the correct letter name in the box below each note. You will find that the letters make words. See the sample.

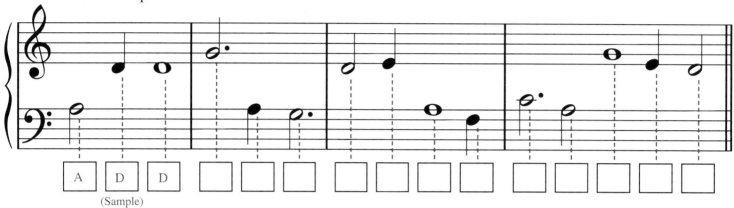

A D D ☐ ☐ ☐ ☐ ☐ ☐ ☐ ☐ ☐ ☐ ☐ ☐

(Sample)

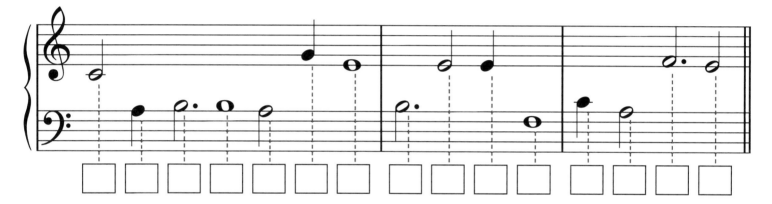

☐ ☐ ☐ ☐ ☐ ☐ ☐ ☐ ☐ ☐ ☐ ☐ ☐ ☐

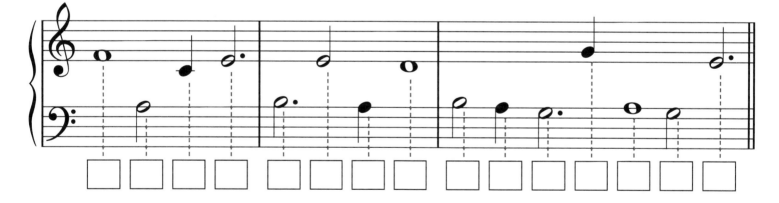

☐ ☐ ☐ ☐ ☐ ☐ ☐ ☐ ☐ ☐ ☐ ☐ ☐ ☐ ☐

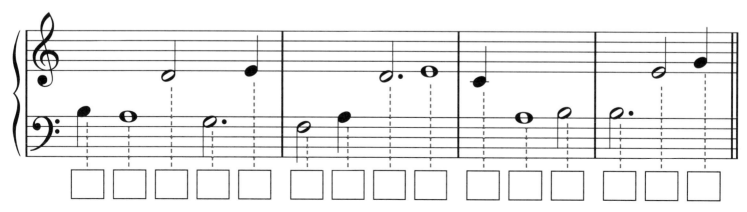

☐ ☐ ☐ ☐ ☐ ☐ ☐ ☐ ☐ ☐ ☐ ☐ ☐ ☐

* Teacher's Note: Do not explain note values or counting in this lesson. Measure bar lines are used to separate the different words. Time signatures have been omitted intentionally. A mixture of notes is used to simulate actual note reading.

Lesson 27. Expanded Note Reading

Name _____ Date _____ Grade _____

New notes in the bass staff and in the treble staff are labeled with red letters in the keyboard chart.

DIRECTIONS: Write the correct letter name in the box below each note. You will find that the letters make words. See the sample.

C D E F

G A B C

E | G | G

(Sample)

Lesson 28. Sharps, Flats and Naturals

Name _____   Date _____   Grade _____

DIRECTIONS: Write S (sharp) below each sharp sign. Write F (flat) below each flat sign. Write N (natural) below each natural sign.

This sign (♯) is a SHARP.
This sign (♭) is a FLAT.
This sign (♮) is a NATURAL.

The center part of a *sharp or natural* looks like a box. The center part of a *flat* looks like a heart shape cut in half. The *center parts* are placed on a staff line or space, like the round part of a note.

DIRECTIONS: Fill in the *center part* of each sharp, flat and natural in the two staffs below.

DIRECTIONS: Write the correct letter name in the box below each sharp, flat and natural. The *center part* tells you the letter name.

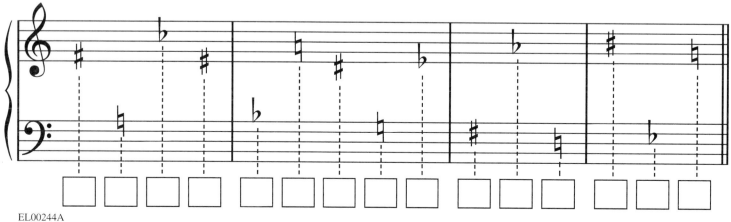

EL00244A

Lesson 29. A Musical Story

Name _____   Date _____   Grade _____

The missing words in this story can be found by identifying the letter names of the notes. *Watch carefully!* Some notes are in the *treble* staff; others are in the *bass* staff.

DIRECTIONS: Write the correct letter name below each note. You will find that the letters make words to complete the story.

THE HUNGRY DOG

One day Laddie, the beautiful collie dog, looked up at his master's

---- ---- ---- ----
(Write letter names)

and ____ to be ____ . So ____

asked his ____ for money to buy ____ for Laddie.

Then ____ hurried to the store and came back with a ____ of

____ . Laddie's ____ was six months, and he was not a

____ dog, even though he got into mischief now and then. After his ____ ,

Laddie took a little nap in his ____ . While the dog was ____ ,

____ sat nearby and looked lovingly at Laddie's ____ .

Lesson 30. Eighth Note Pairs

Name _____ Date _____ Grade _____

Here are two pairs of 8th notes. Notice that each pair is
connected by a thick line, called a *beam*.

* Two 8th notes equal the value of one quarter note.
  The following sample shows how to count 8th notes in $\frac{4}{4}$ time.

  Eighth notes are also counted this way in $\frac{2}{4}$ and $\frac{3}{4}$ time.

DIRECTIONS: Write the counting number below each note. If necessary, refer to Lessons 20, 21 and 22.

* Teacher's Note: The plus sign (+) is an abbreviation of *and*. If you prefer, *and* could be abbreviated with the letter a or by an ampersand (&).

EL00244A